SHOOT

your

SHOT

PURSUING THE PRESENCE OF JESUS

JOHN COBB II

Shoot your Shot
©2021 John Cobb
Published by: John Cobb

ISBN: 978-0-578-32965-9
Library of Congress number: 2021923509

Edited by: Keyoka Kinzy
Cover and Interior Layout: Write on Promotions

Dedication

I want to first thank and acknowledge God for giving me the Grace, Faith, and the Ability to complete this assignment. This was not the easiest journey but well worth the push. Thanks be to God, who gives us the victory through our Lord Jesus Christ. I'm forever grateful for the manifested presence, love, and power of Jesus Christ for making this possible.

To the love of my life and mother of our four children, Alexandria Cobb. You made sure that I kept my focus and prayed me through the process. You believed in me when I thought I couldn't complete this book. These 7 years of marriage have been the most fun and fulfilling years of my life even in the toughest times. I love and appreciate you forever! To my 4 babies Isaiah, Joel, Destini, and Gracelyn Raine who call me daddy and Pastor. You four bring so much joy. I look forward to walking through the door of our home just to be stampede while hearing daddy, daddy, daddy's home. Daddy love you so much.

I dare not forget my mother: Pamela Towns, mom you did an outstanding job raising four children as a single parent. I've seen you work so hard to make sure we had and our home was taken care of. You are a woman worth celebrating. Thank you so much for making sure I didn't end this year without writing my first book. I'm so thankful God chose you to be my mom. I love you so much!

I dare not forget my Pastors, Apostle Travis and Pastor Stephanie Jennings thank you for every push, prophecy, and prayer. You both are amazing leaders. It's an honor being a submitted son. I love you immensely.

Lastly but definitely not least I want to thank the covenant partners of The Turning Point Ministries a church like no other. I appreciate every vision partner, son, and daughter of the ministry for your continued support in Turning Hearts Back To God. I sincerely thank you for all of your love and support.

Jude 1:25 to the only wise God our Saviour, be glory and majesty, dominion and power, both now and ever. Amen

Introduction

Prayer is the source of life. It should be our lifeline. Prayer is not something that we cannot survive without. Prayer is like breathing. It connects us to the heart and mind of God. It's in Him that we live move and have our being. It becomes oxygen to our spirit. We feel a source of life and connected to God when we pray. Prayer brings us out of a dry place into a saturated place. A life of prayer increases our desperation for the manifested presence of the living God. There is a level in prayer that reaches beyond breakthrough atmospheres. This is why it's imperative to press pass our flesh, emotions, and even our own energy, there is a glory that goes beyond the excitement of spiritual momentum that becomes even more unprecedented. God then start to trust us with more because we've developed the kind of maturity in prayer that understands prayer as being much more than a means for us to convince God to grant us our requests.

We have to understand that prayer is a place where we encounter God and know the realities of His kingdom. It is when we mature in prayer that we prioritize prayer over any and everything God could give us. Often times we'll find ourselves praying not to receive anything, but to get lost in the awe of God's majesty. We pray fervently because we have come to know a rest that we can labor to enter into (Hebrews 4:11). Instead of getting discouraged with the lack of results we believe we are experiencing, we should give more attention to and place more value on the tangible presence can create breakthrough atmospheres and manifestations even beyond what you believe for.

It is in an atmosphere of His presence that the revelation and instruction comes that leads us into manifestation of what we are praying for. We learn to cooperate with this reality and we only do so with experience. Sometimes the tangible presence of God will completely change the manner in which we are praying. At other times the revelation that comes in the atmosphere will change our perspective about what we are praying. There is also times when the atmosphere in prayer provokes us in embracing global prayer concerns. We should embrace the shifting in realization that as we pray God's concerns He will take care of ours.

SHOOT *your* SHOT

From Experience to Encounters

There are amazing benefits to seeking God and encountering His Spirit. Not only will you have a prayer life, but you are about to have experiences and encounters with the Spirit of God. Prayer without the Spirit of God and the presence of God yields no results. We are wasting our breath. We are burning ourselves out. It is only in an encounter, or in the presence of God, where our eyes will be open. The Bible says, "For God knows that when you eat from it your eyes will be opened and you will be like God knowing good and evil" (*New International Version,* Gen. 3:5). Through an encounter with God, your eyes will be blessed to see.

"Call unto me, and I will answer thee, and show thee great and mighty things, which thou know not (Jeremiah 33:3). In the presence of God, He will open your eyes and show you something more. I do not know about you but I long for more of God! "As a deer pants for streams of water, so my soul pants for you, my God" (Psalm 42:1). Rivers are not released until the Holy Spirit shows up and releases them.

Say this: I do not just want to experience God; I want to encounter His Spirit. If we really mean this, then it is imperative that we prioritize His presence above everything else. You must be presence-driven. An encounter is the Holy Spirit's doing and an experience is our doing. When you are in prayer and in the presence of God, do not let the end of your prayer be the point of breakthrough. Do not stop at the point of your breakthrough. Allow God to mark you in that moment by staying in His presence. This measure of presence will be the only thing that can truly penetrate the dense darkness of the heart and the only thing that satisfies a hungry heart for more of God. You must be willing to pay the price in the secret place to get His presence to mark you.

Many people will pray, then when God gives them what they want, they leave prayer behind. No, you should stay there until He gives you what you need. Do not move out of the posture of prayer when the presence of God is made known to you, or when you feel like your prayer has been heard, or when you know it has been answered. The Spirit of God allows us to become aware of the presence of God. The key to an encounter with the Holy Spirit is to wait long enough – wait beyond the tears, beyond the worship, beyond how you feel. Then, something deeper will take place. The Bible says, "...weeping may endure for a night, but joy cometh in the morning" (Psalm 30:5).

David said, "I waited patiently." In Psalm 40:1, "I waited patiently for the LORD; and he inclined unto me and heard my cry." David waited with expectancy. As a result, the Lord inclined his ear. He listened intentionally and attentively, and He was receptive to David's cry. Just as the Holy Spirit is intentional about hearing our cries, we must be intentional about hearing His instructions, His will for our life, and His heart. If you want to encounter the presence of God, then you must wait patiently.

Patience is the supernatural fruit of the Holy Spirit. Refer to 1 Samuel to understand that lack of patience can cause you to miss blessings. Being patient is a vital part of trusting in God. "The Lord is good to those who wait for Him, to the soul who seeks Him (Lam. 3:25). When we wait on God, it places us in a position of submission and dependency on Him.

"God is always God (Psalm 46:10), but the Bible says to "be still and know that He is God." I have found that I experience God's presence the most when I quietly wait upon Him. As we sit quietly in God's presence, we can meditate on His Word.

6

Sometimes, His Word will can come alive to us (Psalm 1:1-3).

We live in a distracted culture, where there is always noise. Many times, we just need to sit at the feet of Jesus. The pursuit of God's presence is a powerful element in our lives. It requires discipline, deliberate focus, and effort. "God is worthy of our undivided attention" (Matt. 6:34 MSG). Expectancy is what drives me to wait on the presence of Holy Spirit. "My soul waits thou only upon God for my expectation is from Him (*King James Version,* Psalm 62:5). While you wait expectantly on the presence of Holy Spirit, visualize Jesus performing what you expect from Him. Your expectation breeds results.

While you are in the presence of God, He will take you from where you are into where He wants you to be. He takes you into His supernatural world. The more you spend time in God's presence, the more His presence will become your presence.

Sometimes, we may want the "laying on of hands" in Hebrews 6:2 to be our job, but it's honestly up to God to do all the touching. The stronger the presence of God is, the more there's a release of God's power. It encompasses any distance between the person releasing the impartation and the person receiving the impartation. For example, in Mark 16:17, the apostles began releasing power by "the laying on of hands," but by Acts 5:15, even

Peter's shadow carries the power. God wants to demonstrate His glory through each and every one of us. "For I reckon that the sufferings of this present time are not worthy to be compared with the glory which shall be revealed in us" (Rom. 8:18). The glory cannot be revealed in us without the Holy Spirit in us.

Glory is mentioned 375 times in the King James Bible. The first time the word "glory" is mentioned in the Scripture, it represents wealth. The Shekinah glory represents the physical and visible manifestation of God. Finally, the kabod represents the heaviness and tangibility of God's manifest presence. Glory has represented strength and it has also represented honor in the Scripture. Glory is dimensional. The more you sing, worship, and pray, the more you sense and feel the presence of God.

The infilling of the Spirit of God is where the presence and power of God is accessed (Acts 1:8, 2:4). There is a difference between the presence and power of God. The presence of God is understood in the existence of who God is, but the power of God is understood in the experience of what God can perform.

JOHN COBB II

It's a Different

World

There is a remnant arising, who does not just want the hype. They want the authentic presence of God. They want an encounter with God. The Holy Spirit spoke to me and said, "The days of experimenting are over, and the days of encounters are here. You are about to know God in ways you have never known Him before." My prayer is that your hunger for God is stirred as you read this book. The Bible says, "What no eye has seen, what no ear has heard, and what no human mind has conceived, the things God has prepared for those who love Him" (*New International Version*, 1 Cor. 2:9). Our motive for pursuing God must be to know Him and not to use Him for what He can do. God wants a relationship with you.

The Holy Spirit wants to invite you into His world. He wants to lead and guide you into all the truth. The Bible says, "For all who are led by the Spirit of God are the sons of God" (Rom. 8:14). As I told you previously, it is the Spirit of God that makes us aware of the presence of God. It is the Spirit of God that administers the power of God. We cannot seek the power of God without first seeking His presence. For the power of God to be released into our lives, the presence of God is required. Acts 1:8 says, "[We] receive power when the Holy Spirit comes on you." The Holy Spirit wants us to know more about who He is, more about His world, more about His power, and more about who He created us to be. "That I may know Him, and the power of His resurrection, and the fellowship of His sufferings, being made conformable unto His death" (*King James Version*, Philippians 3:10).

When you are going through a rough time, Jesus Christ hurts with you. But this is an opportunity, an invitation, to know him better. Suffering is a call to intimacy with Jesus. When you walk through difficult things with the Lord, it results in a resurrection from the dead. When Apostle Paul talks about resurrection, he's not only talking about being risen from the dead, although that will happen. Paul is talking about experiencing Jesus' power to resurrect in this life, to joyously overcome every challenge. Paul desired an "outside-the-box" encounter of the living Christ, who operated in and through his life. The Spirit of God encourages us to come from where we are to where He is. You have to be willing to depart. Leave what's comfortable in order to get to the Promised Land. The Bible says, " Then the Lord said to Moses, "Leave this place, you and the people you brought up out of Egypt, and go up to the land I promised on oath to Abraham, Isaac and Jacob, saying, 'I will give it to your descendants'" (Exodus 33:1).

It is imperative that the people of God know and understand the supernatural. If the Church does not understand the supernatural, or if we are afraid of the supernatural, we will be at a disadvantage against the power of ignorance, fear, and deception. It says in 2 Corinthians 2:11, "Lest Satan should take advantage of us: for we are not ignorant of his devices."

The enemy's only leverage to overstep God-given authority is ignorance. In 1 Corinthians 12, Apostle Paul urges us to not be ignorant of spiritual things and of the supernatural because God wants us to grow up in the maturity of the Word and the Spirit. So, when we do not understand the supernatural, the enemy has the advantage. "My people are destroyed for the lack of knowledge. Because you have rejected knowledge, I also reject you as my priests; because you have ignored the law of your God, I also will ignore your children" (Hosea 4:6).

Even now, there is a growing hunger and awareness of spiritual things. Habakkuk 2:14 promises that there is going to be a continuous growing demand for "...the knowledge of the glory of God." There will always be a demand for the supernatural here on earth. God wants us to know more about who He is, more about His world, and more about His power. Only then will we learn more about who He created us to be.

Many people try to relate to God through external means only. They have not been taught that they can know God in a deeper way. In other words, their relationship with God is revolved around thinking about going to heaven, getting their needs met, asking God to deliver them out of danger. The Bible says, "Deep calls to deep" (Psalm 42:7).

All of God, the great I am, lives in all of those who have received Jesus Christ and He has wonderful things in mind for you as you respond to the deeper things of His kingdom. Our relationship with God can and should be more meaningful. We can know His personality, we can know his friendship, we can know his voice, we can know his heart and we have even been invited to know and understand his world. We can't embrace one side of the supernatural. Some people only want to have supernatural encounters and experience God, but the most important thing is that we become like him, transformed into His likeness.

Transformation is key. When we are transformed, His ways become our ways. If we want to know God's world, then we cannot "...conform to the pattern of this world, but be transformed by the renewing of [our] mind" (Romans 12:2). That is the only way you can prove what is good, acceptable, and the perfect will of God. When you conform to the kingdom of God, you are transformed by His Spirit. Zechariah 4:6 says, "...Not by might nor by power, but by my Spirit."

When we are transformed by His Spirit, His thoughts become our thoughts. Don't believe me? Let's look to the Word.

"Let this mind be in you, which was also in Christ Jesus" (Philippians 2:5).

"But we all, with open face beholding as in a glass the glory of the Lord, are changed into the same image from glory to glory" (2 Cor. 3:18).

"For those who are led by the Spirit of God are the children of God" (Rom. 8:14).

"Through these he has given us his very great and precious promises, so that through them you may participate in the divine nature" (2 Peter 1:4).

Let's look at Enoch, for example. Enoch was so supernatural that he lived and walked in two worlds at the same time. In Genesis 5:24, it says, "Enoch walked faithfully with God; then he was no more, because God took him away." He was humane enough to walk on the earth, but spiritual enough to access heaven and walk with God at the same time.

Heaven is the kingdom that God created. Earth is an extension of His kingdom and built as a reflection of it. When God created earth, He decided that Man would rule there as part of His eternal family. In Matthew 6:10, it reads "...on earth as it is in heaven." God wanted there to be constant interaction between heaven and earth. The kingdom of God is, in fact, an open heaven within the earth.

As the Church, we are beyond excited to go to heaven one day. We are excited about bringing heaven down into earth. Romans 15 teaches us that the kingdom of God is an atmosphere in the Holy Ghost. This means that when we receive the Holy Spirit, we do not receive only a person, but we also receive an entire kingdom. In Luke 12, Jesus teaches that the kingdom of God is within us. When we show up, the kingdom of God shows up with us. Its resources become our resources. Its laws become our laws. Its power becomes our power. It's literally called "the power of the world to come" (Hebrew 6:5).

When Jesus entered a city, He always announced that the kingdom of God was at hand. He taught his disciples to do this as well. This means that heaven is always near. Heaven is within arm's reach. Heaven is not just up, it's within and it's always around us. This is the kingdom of God. This is the reality of another world in our world through the power of God's spirit.

God wants things on the earth to be just like they are in heaven. When Adam sinned, mankind was locked out of this dimension. As a result, Man must be born of the spirit to enter the kingdom of God, which is a heavenly dimension on earth.

We are all born spiritually dead because of Adam's sin. We must be willing to allow God to cause us to be reborn by His Spirit. We have to accept the invitation into His world and enjoy an eternal relationship with Him.

When we are born of the water and Spirit, according to John 3:3, we cannot only see the kingdom of God but enter the kingdom of God. John 1 teaches that God gave power to everyone who received His son, Jesus, to become sons of God. As we receive Jesus, we allow His spirit to baptize us and submerse us into the process of being reborn in the spirit. We will begin to see the kingdom of God. We will begin to experience heaven on earth. We have been given the invitation to enter God's world. This is a chance to be with Him and get to know him as our father in heaven.

You don't embrace the miracle; you embrace the miracle worker. We don't get to choose how God manifests when we seek Him. He will always manifest according to the will of the Father. The focus should never be the manifestation. We should have an expectation for manifestation (yes), but we should never focus solely on the manifestation. Whenever we seek God, we should expect Him to manifest Himself. However, we are never seeking manifestations, we are seeking Jesus. Anyone who refuses to embrace this principle can easily open themselves to deception. This is how they can end up entertaining weird or demonic manifestations. When you pursue Jesus, it is the only safe and guaranteed way we can encounter Him in the Supernatural.

If you want to receive, simply seek Jesus and keep falling in love with Him, regardless of what manifestation you experience in the Supernatural. None of the manifestations of the Spirit are better than Him. Jesus is the best thing that could ever happen for us. Once you are in a place where nothing else matters but Jesus, there are various manifestations of the spirit of God that you may become aware of. The Supernatural is a realm in the Spirit. Through the prophetic, you may experience multiple dimensions. The Supernatural isn't scheduled or planned. The Supernatural is the reward for seeking Jesus. The Bible says, "But without faith it is impossible to please him: for he that cometh to God must believe that he is, and that he is a rewarder of them that diligently seek

Him" (Hebrews 11:6). The Supernatural was never meant for just September or just June. The Supernatural is eternal. When you walk in the Spirit, you begin to operate in the Supernatural. Therefore, being filled with Holy Spirit and led by Holy Spirit is important.

When you experience God in the Supernatural, it is about getting to know the Lord Jesus in a real way that extends beyond our initial faith in Him as a believer. There is an invitation to work closely with him on a consistent basis. By becoming the sons and daughters of His kingdom, you can do the works He has done and achieve even greater. "Verily, verily, I say unto you,

He that believeth on me, the works that I do shall He do also; and greater works than these shall He do; because I go unto my Father" (John 14:12). The Scripture teaches that eternal life consists of knowing God (John 17:3). This means to know intimately through experience. Baptism of the Spirit is the gateway into the Supernatural. A lot of us do not have the supernatural power of God. We get stuck in one element of God, and it often tends to be an element of our preference.

There is a divine supernatural and a demonic supernatural. When the Church does not understand or is afraid of the Supernatural, its members will be at a disadvantage against the power of ignorance, fear, and deception. They will miss out on the fullness of the abundant life Jesus promised us in John 10:10. We must understand that God is supernatural. According to Luke 10:19, we have been given authority over the power of the devil through Christ Jesus. It was when the heavens opened that the Spirit of God descended on Jesus in Matt. 3. The Supernatural is all about living a life full of the Holy Ghost. When you're living a life full of the Holy Ghost, you are living under an open heaven. This is what happened to Ezekiel. When the heavens opened up, the Spirit entered him, and he saw visions of God (Ezekiel 1:1).

The Supernatural is more than miracles, signs, and wonders. It is the reality of God and His desire to establish His kingdom among men. When you pray with the Holy Ghost inside of you, it establishes a safeguard around your heart. This protects you against spiritual error and the fascination that attempts to draw believers out of God's will. A strong prayer life will keep your focus on Jesus and not the various spiritual trends that can lead to deception. Why would anyone deny empowerment? As we embrace a lifestyle of praying in tongues, it will increase our capacity to comprehend and experience various dimensions of God in the Supernatural.

Hot Pursuit

The more we pursue the presence of God, the more we will see the glory of God. Personal transformation always transpires in the presence of God's glory. We cannot hide from it because we are afraid or ashamed. We need encounters with the glory of God if we are going to change. His glory challenges any darkness that still resides in our souls. It drives deep darkness and bondage away from us. The Bible says, "Arise, shine, for your light has come, and the glory of the Lord rises upon you. See, darkness covers the earth and thick darkness is over the peoples, but the Lord rises upon you and his glory appears over you.

" (*NIV*, Isaiah 60:1-2).

Sometimes, I believe we underestimate the power of prayer. There is a desperate hunger for revival, but we have neglected the discipline of consistent prayer. We will not see revival until we get in the secret and stay there. As believers, we are required to pay the price in the Secret Place. We need to do this so that the presence of God can mark us and change us. God is looking for people who don't mind seeking Him until they find Him. The Bible says, "Seek the Lord while He may be found; call upon Him while He is near (Isaiah 55:6). The power is not in *saying* all the right things, but when we you begin to seek the Lord, He shows up. In Matt. 6:33, it says, "But seek ye first the kingdom of God, and His righteousness; and all these things shall be added to you." We have to be intentional about pursuing the presence of God. I'm intentionally emphasizing a tenacious, focused pursuit of God and His manifested presence. In Psalm 63:8, David said, "My soul followeth hard after thee." Pursuit requires discipline, deliberate focus, and effort. I prophetically decree and declare that as you are reading this book, God will stir your hungry hearts that cry, "God, I want more of you... at all costs." May your hunger grow and become contagious.

It's so imperative that we have a consistent and stable prayer life. You will never appreciate prayer until you understand what it is, the power of it, and the purpose of it. Prayer is more than just inviting God into your life. Prayer is a dialogue between God and you, especially for those who are his covenant partners. Now, let me say this, You cannot have a covenant without relationship. Prayer involves cries for help. The Bible says, "And the Lord said, I have surely seen the affliction of my people which are in Egypt and have heard their cry by reason of their taskmasters; for I know their sorrows" (Exodus 3:7).

God is looking for those who will pray without ceasing. He's looking for those who will pray with boldness and authority. Prayer was not meant to be left up to the mothers and deacons of the Church. It is the entire church's responsibility. "And said unto them, It is written, My house shall be called the house of prayer; but ye have made it a den of thieves" (Matt. 21:13).The praying church overturns demonic plans. It put angels on assignment, cleanses atmospheres, and creates conditions for the visible invasion of the Word of God into the nations. As spiritual kings and priests on the earth, it is our honor and privilege to govern our whole world through prayer. "And hast made us unto our God kings and priests: and we shall reign on the earth" (Rev. 5:10).

See the early church being unceasing in their prayer? They have devoted themselves to prayer. "And they continued steadfastly in the apostles' doctrine and fellowship, and in breaking of bread, and in prayers" (Acts 2:42)... Prayer is commitment. God is looking for us to commit to praying every day. God has given us the empowerment to speak to Him in an unknown tongue as an alternative means of communication. When you are filled with the Holy Ghost, we are empowered to speak with new tongues.

You must speak in tongues as much as possible throughout the day. Sometimes, we can be so busy, but every minute counts. In 1 Corinthians 14, it says, when you pray in tongues, you edify. Edify means "to build up." Therefore, the more you pray in tongues, the intensity builds in prayer.

Smith Wigglesworth is one of God's historic generals in the faith. It was once suggested to Wigglesworth that he must have spent hours and hours in prayer in order to see the miracles that he had seen in his ministry over the years. Wigglesworth's response, however, was that he often did not spend hours in prayer in one setting. Rather, he had a discipline of praying in tongues or meditating on a scripture every 20 minutes.

Sometimes, you need hours to build in prayer, instead of multiple times throughout the day. You may need to consecrate a day or a couple of days to get away from your busy schedule and put in consistent hours with God. There are times when fervency is not the repetition or aggression that we pray in, but rather, the stillness and the surrender. The intensity is more about when all our passion, focus, and desires are on Jesus. The Bible says, "...in quietness and trust is your strength" (Isaiah 30:15). It's good to pray in tongues as we wait on the Lord to focus our minds. Also, we should pray in tongues to get our minds back in sync if they begin to wonder. Another important point I want to make is that praise should always be the power source of fervent prayer when we are pursuing the presence of God. The joy of the Lord is our strength.

When you wait on the Lord, it often consists of a balance of spiritual disciplines that seem contradictory. The scriptures admonish us to be slow to speak as we come into the presence of God. Yet, we are also instructed to be instant in prayer, which means being able to catch the spontaneity of the wind of God in prayer. There are times in prayer when we need to wait until we feel prompted to pray. According to Psalm 80:18, we wait until God literally gives us what to pray for.

There are times when we must stir ourselves and seek the Lord when His presence is seemingly absent. There are other times when, as soon as we simply yield to the work of the Holy Spirit, He takes over! All of these are disciplines that we must rely on for the Spirit of God to lead us into the balance of as we pray. It is the Spirit of God that allows us to become aware of the presence of God. It is also the Spirit of God that administers the power of God. The reality is many may seek the power of God, but they have no desire for the presence of God. In order for the power of God to be released into our lives, the presence of God is required. This is why Acts 1:8 says we receive power AFTER we receive the Spirit.

Whenever we become aware of God's presence in our lives, it's because Jesus is present. The presence of the Lord is the felt existence of Jesus by way of the Spirit of God. The Bible says, "Now the Lord is that Spirit, and where the Spirit of the Lord is, there is freedom" (2 Cor. 3:17). Jesus is wherever His presence is. It is the Spirit of God that causes the presence of the Lord to become real to us. The presence of the Lord has the power to convert the heart of an unbeliever. "Repent ye therefore, and be converted, that your sins may be blotted out, when the times of refreshing shall come from the presence of the Lord" (Act 3:19).

SHOOT *your* SHOT

Desperate Measures

Each of us has the innate instinct to pray, often before we know God. In crisis and in pain, people often reach past themselves into the invisible realm, hoping to receive favor from a God they hope is there. They are frustrated when they do not receive an answer because something inside of them believes and wants to touch God in those moments of desperation.

The instinct to cry out to God emerged soon after the fall of Adam and Eve. Adam and Eve were in close fellowship with God until sin separated them from His presence. They went from being connected in fellowship to being disconnected. The pain of that separation created a deep cry in all of the humanity that followed. According to Genesis 4:26, men and women, on their own, begin to search for and cry out to God. God did not ignore their cries but responded with His friendship and fellowship.

Friendship and fellowship between God and Man look as unique as each individual. We see the story of Enoch, for example. The Bible says Enoch walked faithfully with God and then God took him away (Genesis 5:21-24). God delighted so much in Enoch fellowship that He superimposed eternity upon him before he ever finished living.

Moses had a different story of fellowship. When he began having face-to-face dialogues with God, Moses would shine with the glory of God afterwards (Exodus 34:29-35).

We can even look at the story of Hannah. She was a quiet but tenacious woman, who desperately wanted a child.

SHOOT *your* SHOT

According to 1 Samuel 1:6, Hannah was barren because God had closed her womb. Her sister-wife, Peninnah, delighted in tormenting her over and over. Hannah was miserable, but this did not stop her from petitioning God year after year for a child. At the temple, she prayed deeply to God, and one day, the priest who was watching her thought she was drunk. Even then, she continued to reach out to God through Eli, the priest, telling him what she wanted.

Due to Hannah's persistence, God responded to her cry, giving her over and above what she had requested. Eli prophesized that she would have what she asked for. Later, she gave birth to a powerful son, the prophet Samuel, who would go on to become the next judge of Israel. Hannah could have become offended by God and the people who taunted her. Anger often stops people from praying. Instead, Hannah did the opposite and drew herself nearer to God. She had some powerful results. Prayer is about connection, and we each connect with God uniquely. God is a personal God, and he is also supernatural. For that reason, we may have encounters in prayer that others will not have. Others may not connect to our experiences. This becomes part of our unique journey with Jesus and is never meant to bring about feelings of condemnation.

When you are desperate for more of God, you are willing to go the distance. You are willing to do what it takes, no matter how long it takes. You can't be desperate for His glory and not get His presence. "O God, thou art my God; early I seek thee; my soul thirsteth for you thee my flesh longeth for thee in a dry and thirsty land, where no water is" (Psalm 63:1). When you want more of God, you become thirsty. You're saying, "I cannot survive without you." That's another dimension of God's glory! When you want more of God, you want to be filled with the Spirit of God. Also, you want to be led by the Spirit of God and walk in the Spirit.

There is more to God than what we know or have learned. The depths of God can only be discovered as we research the Word of God. As we pursue God, He begins to stretch our capacity. We become more adjusted in our walk with His movements, which shift from time to time. God will often shift during times when we are most familiar with how God is moving in our lives. Although God's nature does not change, the methods and avenues of which He moves do change. "Jesus is the same yesterday and today and forever" (*NIV*, Heb. 13:8).

The Supernatural does not make sense to the natural mind. When God told Isaiah that he would do a new thing, He also asked if Isaiah would know it (Isaiah 43:19). In other words, before Isaiah could rationalize what God was going to do, it had already been accomplished. God is able to do things quicker than we are able to figure them out. This is why the Supernatural does not make sense to people who are in the flesh. There is no way to explain how Jesus could spit in the mud and make an eyeball out of it (John 9:6-7). The supernatural realm is so multidimensional that it is almost impossible to completely understand. As Eph. 3:17-20 says, the height, the width, the depth, and the length of God's presence and power. Can only be understood when you are "rooted and established in love." The verse goes on to say that "...this love...surpasses knowledge—that you may be filled to the measure of all the fullness of God."

"A dimension is a world that exists with spheres, levels, and stages. Through the process of revelation, its mysteries are unfolded through visions and the breaking of codes over time." - Bishop Tudor Bismark.

Another definition of dimension is "a world of higher thoughts." If you want different things to happen, you must change your way of thinking. There is no way to explain how Jesus in could walk through walls and then vanish after having a conversation with his disciples" (John 20:26). We might become spiritually stagnant when we attempt to explain God before learning how to flow and move with Him as he moves. We often attempt to explain God in a way that fits our box. God does not live in our boxes. "Yea, they turned back and tempted God, and limited the Holy One of Israel" (Psalm 78:41).

God wants to take you higher and deeper. "But we all, with open face beholding as in a glass the glory of the Lord, are changed into the same image from glory to glory, even as by the Spirit of the Lord"

(2 Cor. 3:18). It is impossible to transcend from one glory into another glory. The glory of God is dimensional and His power is dimensional. One glory can be a greater dimension of glory than another. The glory of God is inside of Jesus Himself.

Many people feel as though God is distant or not answering them. These people are not taking the time to listen to Him. "And it shall come to pass, if thou shalt hearken diligently unto the voice of the Lord thy God, to observe and to do all his commandments which I command thee this day, that the Lord thy God will set thee on high above all nations of the earth" (Deut. 28:1). . When we experience God in the Supernatural, we are getting to know the Lord Jesus in a real way. This extends beyond our initial faith in Him as a believer. There is an invitation to work closely with Him, on a consistent basis as sons and daughters in His kingdom. According to John 14:12, He has done and even greater works. There are benefits to knowing God.

The Scripture teaches, in John 17:3 that eternal life consists of knowing God. The word "know" in the text, literally means "to know intimately through experience." Did you know that according to John 17:21-24, the highest place in the Supernatural is walking in an oneness relationship with the Lord? "And to know the love of Christ, which passeth knowledge, that ye might be filled with all the fullness of God" (Eph. 3:19). According to Col. 1:27, Jesus is inside of us as the hope of glory. When you know Jesus and transform into His image, you will reach the highest realm of the Supernatural. "For those God foreknew he also predestined to be conformed to the image of his Son, that he might be the firstborn among many brothers and sisters" (Rom. 8:29).

Another thing I love about God is that He'll never turn you down when you pursue a relationship with Him. His love for you is not based on where you work, how you look, or what you drive. "But God commendeth his love toward us, in that, while we were yet sinners, Christ died for us" (Rom. 5:8). In fact, here's another one: "For God so loved the world that he gave his only begotten Son, that whosoever believeth in him should not perish, but have everlasting life" (John 3:16).

God is clingy. Yep, that's right. He's clingy. But who wouldn't want Jesus to always be around? God said, "Never will I leave you; never will I forsake you" (Heb. 13:5). He's always around. Everywhere you go, Jesus is there. Psalm 139:8says, "If I go up to the heavens, You are there; if I make my bed in the depths, You are there."

When things become worrisome, we are free to approach God and give Him all the details. God will give us the strength to leave our cares at His table. He will take care of it and provide solutions for us to implement. The Bible says, "Cast thy burdens upon the Lord, and He shall sustain thee: He shall never suffer the righteous to be moved" (Psalm 55:22). Often, people have been hurt by others telling their secrets. Most likely, you have given those people what they can't fix, which leads them into giving your problems to someone else who can't fix it either. Now, your business is everywhere, but where you left it! "The Lord will perfect that which concerneth me: thy mercy, O Lord, endureth forever: forsake not the works of thine own hands" (Psalm 138:8). God will turn your worry into worship and your worship into wonders. Don't worry about anything, instead pray about everything. You must tell God what you need and thank him for all He's done (Philippians 4:6).

When I committed to God, I vowed that I would never let anything separate me from Him. What you are committed to demands accountability. It must be embraced and stewarded. I will let nothing separate me from God. Romans 8:38-39 says, "For I am persuaded that neither death, nor life, nor angels, nor principalities, nor powers, nor things to come, nor height, nor depth, nor any other creature shall be able to separate us from the love of God, which is in Christ Jesus our Lord." There is just you and Jesus. Everything else can fade away. That's a true commitment right there. God loves when He has our undivided attention. When He has our undivided attention, we are focused on Him, and Him only.

Relationship Goals

David was a man of praise and faith. That's David the Hero, David the Warrior, David the Outlaw, David the Sinner, David the King, and David the Victim. No matter which part of David's life you study in Scripture, you'll find David seeking God. In Psalm 63:1, it says, "O God, thou art my God; early will I seek thee." You'll find

David praising God in Psalm 86:12, "I will praise thee, O Lord my God, with all my heart: and I will glorify thy name for evermore". You'll even find David crying out to God in Psalm 18:6, "In my distress I called upon the Lord, and cried out to my God: He heard my voice from His temple, and my cry came before Him, even unto His ears." Often, David would consult God. In 2 Samuel 5:19, David inquired of the Lord, saying, "Shall I go up against the Philistines? Wilt thou deliver them into mine hand?" The Lord replied, "Go up: for I will doubtless deliver the Philistines into thine hand."

Throughout David's life, he translated his daily experiences into songs, poems, and prayers of faith and praise. David was not too embarrassed, or too ashamed, to worship and dance with all his might before God and the Ark of the Covenant. He was not concerned with what it might look like to others. He was not worried about looking cool or kingly. Some people would rather portray to others as if they have a relationship with God. In 2 Tim 3:5, they Bible talks about how folks will act religious, but they will reject the power that could make them godly. Stay away from people like that. I would choose a relationship with God over the spirit of religion any day.

Now, David's relationship with God was not a part-time job. The Bible says, "I will walk before the Lord in the land of the living" (*New International Version*, Psalm 116:9.) David's relationship with God was personal from the time he was a boy until the time of his death.

God wants a relationship with you too. There is nothing more fulfilling than wanting someone who wants you back. God wants to be with you as much as you want to be with Him. This is why He left His Spirit (John 14:15-31). The Holy Spirit is not an "it." He's a Spirit, according to John 4. You don't catch the Holy Spirit. He is a person. He is the very Spirit of Jesus. It's imperative that we understand this. It's not until you begin to treat the Holy Spirit like a person that you'll see your relationship with God develop.

God doesn't won't a one-night stand. John 15:4 says, "Abide in me, and I in you. As the branch cannot bear fruit of itself, except it abide in the vine; no more can ye, except ye abide in me." God is asking you to live in Him. He wants an eternal relationship with you. What is an eternal relationship? It's a relationship without a beginning or and an ending. It lasts forever. In John 3:16, it says, "For God so loved the world that He gave His only begotten Son, that whosoever believeth in Him shall not perish, but have eternal life." God wants to talk with you, be with you, dwell in you, and walk with you. "This I say then, Walk in the spirit, and ye shall not fulfill the lust of the flesh" (Gal. 5:16.) Some people pray every now and then. They pray when they need something from God. 1 Thess. 5:11 tells us to never stop praying. They only worship when things are going the way they want them to. Their worship is conditional. God loves you unconditionally. God demonstrates His love for us. While we were still sinners, Christ died for us. Our relationship with God can and should be more meaningful.

The more you pursue Him, the more you will want Him. "God—you're my God! I can't get enough of you! I've worked up such hunger and thirst for God, traveling across dry and weary deserts. So here I am in the place of worship, eyes open, drinking in your strength and glory. In your generous love I am really living at last! My lips brim praises like fountains. I bless you every time I take a breath; My arms wave like banners of praise to you"

(*The Message*, Psalm 63:1-4). This type of draw and attention to Jesus is only triggered in those who have authentically encountered Jesus. There is no marketing that can replace word of mouth. When people love something they have experienced, they tell others about it. When people truly experience Jesus for who He really is, it will create a global demand for His presence and power. People will stand in long lines, camp out overnight, and take extreme measures to be in a place where the presence and power of Jesus is authentically encountered. An encounter with Jesus will have you coming back for more.

"Thou wilt shew me the path of life: in thy presence is fullness of joy; at thy right hand pleasures for evermore" (Psalm 16:11). You'll begin to encounter the joy of the Lord, the fullness of His joy. This joy is so unspeakable and full of glory. You won't be able to put into words what you have encountered. "For the earth shall be filled with the knowledge of the glory of the Lord, as the waters covers the sea" (Hab.2:14). This means the knowledge of the glory cannot be exhausted. Its knowledge is vast. We cannot explain God's glory because it's never ending. The glory is not an encounter we have at a conference. The glory of God is found only in the person of Jesus Christ (2 Cor. 4:6). Glory is dimensional. The glory represents the fullness of God. When we try to explain the glory, we limit ourselves from experiencing the different dimensions of glory. The glory represents everything God is and everything He can do. When pursuing Jesus, you sow in tears but reap in joy (Psalm 126:5.)

In pursuing a relationship with Jesus, we must be intentional. When we are intentional about our relationship with Jesus, we begin to encounter Him in ways we've never encountered Him before. When I'm intentional, I don't have to be reminded to pray, to study His word, or meditate on the Word of God. God is intentional about us. Why can't we be intentional about Him? The Bible says, "And It shall come to pass, that before they call, I will answer; and while they are yet speaking, I will hear" (Isaiah 65:24). It's imperative that you are intentional about your relationship with

Jesus. When you're intentional, you worship Him in Spirit and in truth. "God is a Spirit: and they that worship Him must worship Him in spirit and truth" (John 4:24). If you are really intentional about the things of God, you will have a desperation, a deliberate focus, and an effort for the things of God. You are willing to strengthen your relationship with Him, no matter what it takes.

When we try to please Man, we treat our relationship with God as if He needs us – not as though we need Him. 1 Corinthians 10:31 says, "So whether you eat or drink or whatever you do, do it all for the glory of God." Intentionality breeds intimacy. Our intimate relationship of Jesus leads us to a revelation of our identity as worshipers. A worshipper is an identity that every single believer of Jesus Christ has access to – whether or not you can sing. When you want to embrace your identity in Jesus as a worshipper, it takes abiding. Abiding is when you spend time in the presence of God. "Abide in me, and I in you. As the branch cannot bear fruit of itself, except it abide in the vine; no more can ye, except ye abide in me" (John 15:4). Above anything else, God wants our hearts. Our hearts are the seats of our emotions, willpower, and intellect, which is rooted in who He is. Our hearts need to be rooted in Jesus. Our hearts drive our identity, mindset, passions, and decisions. We must spend time with God, so He can reprogram our hearts.

Apostle Peter had a deep and intimate relationship with the Holy Spirit. According to Acts 5:15, when Peter walked down the street, people were healed in the presence of his shadow. Peter lived in the embrace of the Spirit of God. He was overshadowed by the glory of the presence of the Holy Spirit. What overshadowed him in turn overshadowed the people he encountered. Prayer is an art, meaning it has many different unique facets. All prayer = different types of prayer with different results.

Many have built their relationship with God based on what they've seen in other relationships. It is very easy to see what you want to see. Be careful who you pattern your relationship after. Be careful what you call "relationship goals." What you see is not always what you get. Some people have paid a great price for where they are. Everyone has a story to tell. Everyone who's smiling isn't necessarily happy. No relationship is perfect. The good news is that Jesus is our perfect model of who to relate to and embrace God. Jesus teaches us that the best way to relate to God is to pursue God. He will stretch our capacity and make us more readily able to adjust in our walk with Him. His moves will shift from time to time.

One thing I love about God is that he never changes. The Bible says, "Jesus Christ is the same yesterday and today and forever" (Heb. 13:8). When we know what to expect in our relationship, it can become boring. Likewise, going to the same place every date night can also become boring. You have to change it up sometimes. Change is good. Your relationship with Jesus will never become boring. We have to remember that God often shifts on us. In times when we think we are getting more familiar with Him, He moves in our lives differently. Although God's nature does not change, the methods and avenues he moves through do change. In order to build a solid relationship, consistent communication is key. There is a tremendous amount of power in communication.

What does consistent communication look like? 1 Thess. 5:17, "Pray without ceasing." One translation says, "Never stop praying." When there is no consistent communication, there is disaster. "And he spake a parable unto them to this end, that men ought always to pray, and not to faint" (Luke 18:1). When we do not communicate with God consistently, we do not honor, respect, and acknowledge Him. Our prayers are strictly provisionally-based, need-based, trial or crisis-based. These prayers are a response to an emotion and called "temporal prayers." Conversations have power to build trust, create meaning, and engage others. How can I trust someone I've barley communicated with? "Trust in the Lord with all thine heart and lean not unto thine own understanding" (Proverbs 3:5).

When you don't communicate with God, you're saying, "I can do this by myself. I don't need Him." Conversations allow for learning and provide a basis for understanding to occur. We honor God by coming to Him with a desire to be in relationship with Him, by wanting to speak with Him, acknowledging that He alone is God by saying good things to Him. For instance, I tell God, "Father, you are good. Father, you are a wonderful God. There is no one like you." Your words of praise, thanksgiving, and affirmation will help you give God the rightful position in your heart. Women love to feel like the only woman that exists. Men like to be praised for their accomplishments and feel loved. So does God. "For thou shalt worship no other god: for the Lord, whose name is Jealous, is a jealous God" (*New International Version,* Exodus 34:14).

"Whatever it is that we may experience, and however we may be broken, God has a good end in store for us."

- Dr. Charles Stanley.

"Beloved, I wish above all things that thou mayest prosper and be in health, even as thy soul prospereth" (3 John 1:2). Not only does God want what's best for you, but He knows what's best for you. According to Isaiah 55:9, "For as the heavens are higher than the earth, so are my ways higher than your ways, and my thoughts than your thoughts." Getting a raise in income, getting a promotion, getting a degree, or improving your fitness are all fine with Him. But these things are only beneficial as your

soul prospers. Without a prospering soul –
that is, without spiritual development –
your motivations will be misplaced. Your
health and wealth will leave you hollow.
You have to trust that God has your best
interests at heart. "Be still, and know that
I am God: I will be exalted among the
heathen, I will be exalted in the earth (*King
James Version*, Psalm 46:10). You have to
be confident in knowing that God wants to
see you win. "Being confident of this very
thing, that He which hath begun a good
work in you will perform it until the day of
Jesus Christ" (Philippians 1:6). "For I know
the thoughts that I think towards you saith
the Lord thoughts of peace and not of evil

to give you an expected end" (Jeremiah 29:11).

"Howbeit when he, the Spirit of truth, is come, he will guide you into all truth: for he shall not speak of Himself; but whatsoever he shall hear, that shall he speak: and will shew you things to come" (John 16:13). God doesn't sugar coat anything. Psalm 19:7 confirms that the instructions of the Lord are perfect for reviving the soul. These are the decrees of the Lord, which are trustworthy and make the wise something simple. Now, you have to be ready for the truth. Some of us rather hear a lie than the truth. God wants to free you, and your freedom comes from Him telling you the truth. He's not concerned about sparing our feelings. "Cry aloud, spare not, lift up thy voice like a trumpet, and shew my people their transgression, and the house of Jacob their sins" (Isaiah 58:1).

SHOOT *your* SHOT

————

Kingdom Agenda

When we preach about Jesus and how He offers salvation, He provides confirmation through miracles. He does this with His Spirit. "Then He answered and spake unto me, saying, this is the word of the Lord unto Zerubbabel, saying, not by might, nor by power, but by my spirit, saith the Lord of hosts" (Zechariah 4:6). People then know He is alive because they realize that He is still performing miracles they have heard about from the Bible. Everyone who believes Jesus is alive can be changed in His nature and become a citizen of His Kingdom. They can enjoy the benefits of His kingdom, as their legal right in this life and in the life to come. This is what we preach.

The kingdom is not exclusive to the blood of Jesus, the cross, and the resurrection. These are a means of entrance into the Kingdom of God. There is only one gospel. "For I am not ashamed of the gospel of Christ: for it is the power of God unto salvation to everyone that believeth; to the Jews first, and also to the Greek" (Romans 1:16). There is only one gospel of the Kingdom of God, but many messages. The power of God is for now. When we preach, we should look for an all-out invasion of heaven that verifies what we are preaching. We're not waiting until we make it to heaven, but heaven is invading the earth every time we share Jesus with others. "And Jesus came and spake unto them, saying 'All power is given unto me in heaven and in earth'" (Matt. 28:18).

God is out of the box. He's not even limited to the four walls of the church. God wants the church to take His Supernatural power to the world. "Let all the earth fear the Lord: let all the inhabitants of the world stand in awe of Him" (Psalm 33:8). Ezekiel had a prophetic encounter in Ezekiel 47. In his vison, the further the waters flowed from the temple, the deeper the waters became. The more the Church takes the Supernatural power of God outside the walls of the church and to the Lost, the deeper the anointing will become. This is one of the keys to operating in a greater dimension of God's power. We have to take the power to the Lost. The truth is that God wants the rivers to flow outside of the temple and not exclusively inside of the temple. When the waters deepened, it represented how the flow of God's power intensifies in our lives the more we reach out to the Lost. The Scriptures also indicates, in Ezekiel 47 that as the waters became deeper, there is healing for the nations. This represents a move of God's Spirit and power that will come through the Church as we reach those who are lost.

The joy in the city of Sameria came with a great price. Stephen lost his life for preaching the gospel of the kingdom. The Jewish leaders couldn't stand to hear Stephen any longer. The Bible says that they covered their ears, dragged Stephen out of the city, and stoned him to death. We live in a season where many have covered their ears to keep from hearing the truth. They rather be bound to a lie than to be set free by the truth. John 8:32 says, "And ye shall know the truth, and the truth shall make you free." While he was being stoned, Stephen called on Jesus, saying, "Lord Jesus, receive my spirit." Then, he got on his knees and cried out, saying, "Lord, don't charge them with this sin," and died. He was praying for their forgiveness. After Stephen's stoning, witnesses laid their clothes at the feet of Saul.

The Bible says, "And ye shall hear of wars and rumors of wars: see that ye be troubled: for all these things must come to pass, but the end is not yet" (Matt. 24:6). This is the beginning of something great. "That the trail of your faith, being much more precious than of gold that perisheth, though it be tried with fire, might be found unto praise and honor and glory at the appearing of Jesus Christ" (1 Peter 1:7). You rejoice in this. Nothing should produce greater joy than knowing your security in Jesus Christ. That's true even if you suffer grief of various trials. Your ability to cope in the present is tied to your understanding of your inheritance in the future. If you cannot make a link between the now (trials and sufferings) and the not yet (eternal glory), grace won't be multiplied in your life. God allows trails to refine your faith, like gold, so that it may result in the praise of Jesus. All trials are designed to do three things: prove your faith, develop your faith, and glorify God. You will never know what you believe until you have faced a test. The heavenly goldsmith wants to refine your character. How should we respond while living in times of trials? We need to love Jesus Christ, believe Jesus Christ, and rejoice in Jesus Christ.

Isaiah 43:19 says, "Behold, I will do a new thing; now it shall spring forth; shall ye not know it? I will even make a way in the wilderness, and rivers in the desert." I know what you are experiencing now may be treacherous territory, but the Spirit of the Lord goes before you now to make a way. Expect God to move in unexpected ways. All too often, instead of maintaining an attitude of expectancy, we get caught up in the appearance of the situation. Now is not the time to lose heart. God is getting you ready for a greater blessing than you were expecting. "But the God of all grace, who hath called us unto His eternal glory by Christ Jesus, after that ye have suffered a while, make you perfect, stablish, strengthen, settle you" (1Peter 5:10). God is going to exceed your expectations. You're being positioned for a major breakthrough. "Now unto him that is able to do exceedingly abundantly above all that we ask or think, according to the power that worketh in us" (Eph. 3:20).

I pray that your hunger is stirred for more of God. Many will testify that reading this book is the Lord's doing and it will be marvelous in our eyes. I want to encourage you to keep pursuing the presence of Jesus. Live a life that revolves around pursuing Him. Let this be your lifeline. The more you pursue Him, the more He will reveal who He is to you. Isaiah 55:6 says, "Seek ye first the Lord while He may be found, call upon Him while He is near." Keep seeking Him, even when He answers. "Therefore, my beloved brethren, be ye steadfast, unmovable, always abounding in the work of the Lord, forasmuch as ye know that your labor is not in vain in the Lord" (1 Corinthians 15:58). Say this loud, "KEEP GOING!"

Your prayers aren't in vain; your worship isn't in vain; your witness isn't in vain; your servitude isn't in vain. This is one relationship where you don't have to feel like you are not good enough. "And let us not be weary in well doing: for in due season we shall, reap, if we faint not (Gal. 6:9). Don't fret but keep pursuing Him. "I had fainted, unless I had believed to see the goodness of the Lord in the land of the living" (Psalm 27:13). Some people define their relationship with Jesus by prayer and going to church on Sundays. That's it. It takes much more than that. Prayer and church is a start, but just a start. We have to spend time with Him Sunday through Saturday, 365 days a year. We have to embrace and accept Him for who He is. We have to cater to Him through our honor, praise, and worship.

There is a growing hunger and awareness of spiritual things. This is because God wants to show us something. He wants us to you who He is, more about His world, more about His power, and more about who He created us to be. Most people attempt to relate to God through external means. People who do this have not been taught that they can know God in a deeper way. Their only relationship with God is in thinking about going to heaven, getting their needs met, asking Him to rescue them out of trouble, and helping them in life. Our relationship with God should be more meaningful. We can know His personality; we can know His friendship; we can know His voice; we can know His heart and His world (the Supernatural).

The Bible says, "He that dwellth in the secret place of the most high shall abide under the shadow of the almighty" (Psalm 91:1). What better time to embrace Jesus and let Him embrace you than right now? There is a such thing as cuffing season. For those of us who don't know what cuffing season is, it refers to a specific time of year. As the temperature drops, the number of couples rise. "Draw nigh to God, and He will draw nigh to you" (James 4:8). When you draw near to God, you can come into His presence with prayer, praise, and obedience. This goes beyond a Sunday experience. When you are really thirsty for more of God, you desire more than an experience. You want can encounter. We cannot expect to have a revival if the place of encounter is replaced.

"Revival requires an encounter, and an encounter requires intentional time, effort, and the priority to find his space and encountering His face." - Pastor Kim Owens.

"The Lord hath appeared of old unto me, saying, Yea, I have loved thee with an everlasting love: therefore with love and kindness have I drawn thee" (Jer. 31:3). We are drawn close to Him by reflecting the love shown by Him, shown to Him. Secondly, you must resist the devil. There is only one way to resist the devil. It's the same way Jesus did by using the Word of God. When the devil tells his lies to your conscience, proclaim the truth of the Word of God. The devil will flee from you. But you can't proclaim what you don't know. Third, live a life of repentance. Cleanse your hands and purify your hearts. Some people don't receive the help they need from God because they "don't sin." They make "mistakes," but didn't die for the mistakes; He died for sins. We live in a culture that rejects personal responsibility and downplays sin. Those are symptoms of pride, which takes us right back to where James started and where he ends. Humble yourselves before the Lord and He will exalt you. Admit your sin and eradicate pride.

God's got you!

"I will say of the Lord, He is my refuge and my fortress: my God, in Him will I trust" (Psalm 91:2). Has someone ever told you that they had your back and you allowed them to carry you, but they dropped you? They said they would protect you, but they let someone hurt you. If God says He's got you, you can trust that He's got you. . You don't have to worry about

102

God dropping you. No weapon formed against you shall prosper, but every tongue that rises up against in judgement of you will be condemned. Some of us keep getting hurt because we allow people, who aren't allowing Holy Spirit to carry them, carry us. Now, you're hurt and blaming God. "But Jesus beheld them, and said unto them, with men this impossible; but with God all things are possible" (Matt. 19:26). He wasn't saying that it couldn't be done. He was saying that it can't be done effectively without Him. My prayer is that you desire to know God in a greater way.

Shoot Your Shot

Jesus left His Spirit here, so that we would always be with Him and He with us. The Bible says, "I will not leave you comfortless: I will come to you. Yet a little while, and the world seeth me no more; but ye see me: because I live, ye shall live also. At that day ye shall know that I am in my Father, and ye in me, and I in you" (John 14:18). He loves you that much. God loves you so much that He desires to never be apart from any of us. He wants an intimate relationship with us. So, we must pursue intimacy with Him. We will live our lives by the Holy Spirit when we pursue an interment relationship with Jesus. You begin to want Him as much as He wants you. You start wanting Him more than your fleshy desires.

Your flesh has the potential to lead you to sin, fear, failures, abandonment, and hell. "This I say then, walk in the Spirit, and ye shall not fulfil the lust of the flesh" (Gal. 5:16). . You need the Spirit of God.

According to Acts 1:8, you must first be filled with Holy Spirit (Power), then you "shall receive power after...the Holy Ghost is come upon you. Then, you must be led by the Spirit (Character) and you are filled with the Holy Spirit. The Bible says, "For as many as are led by the Spirit of God, they are the sons of God (Romans 8:14). Then, you must walk in the Spirit (Supernatural). 1 John 2:6 says, "He that saith he abideth in him ought himself also, so to walk even as He walked." If we want an intimate relationship with God, we must worship Him and spend time with Him in prayer. "But the hour cometh, and now is, when the true worshipers shall worship the

Father in spirit and in truth: for the Father seeketh such to worship Him" (John 4:23).

God is looking for those who would worship and cater to Him. Worship is the submission of all of our nature to God.

"Worship is the submission of all of our nature to God. It is the quickening of the conscience by his holiness; the nourishment of mind with his truth; the purifying of imagination by his beauty; the opening of the heart to his love; the surrender of will to his purpose--all this gathered up in adoration, the most selfless emotion of which our nature is capable." - William Temple"

The word "worship" in Hebrew is *shachah,* which means "to bow in respect and reverence." The Bible says, "Let all the earth fear the Lord: let all the inhabitants of the world stand in awe of Him" (Psalm 33:8). Our lives should bow to the Holy Spirit in respect and reverence. To worship is to encounter God. Encounters with the Holy Spirit lead us to holiness, truth, purity, love, purpose, and surrender.

"Before I formed thee in the belly I knew thee, and before thou camest forth out of the womb I sanctified thee, and I ordained thee a prophet unto thee nations" (Jeremiah 1:5). See, God knew you before you thought you knew yourself. He knows what you are capable of. In Ecc. 1:9, it says, "The thing that hath been, it is that which shall be; and that which is done is that which shall be done: and there is no new thing under the sun." Your mistakes and failures are nothing new to God. This is why you shouldn't follow your heart. You should follow the leading of the Holy Spirit. "The heart is deceitful above all things, and desperately wicked: who can know it?" (Jeremiah 17:9).

Have you ever felt in your heart that the person you liked was The One? That feeling felt so right, but it turned out to be so wrong? You listened to everybody else, instead of the voice of God. Maybe because it wasn't what you wanted to hear. This goes back to God knowing us and because he knows us, He knows what best for us. Not everything we like is what we need. I know they told you to be yourself, but if you keep being yourself when you know yourself is your worst enemy, you'll always be disappointed. If your self doesn't have the Holy Spirit, it will be a danger to you. Be who God has created you to be.

Hebrews 4:16 says, "Let us therefore come boldly unto the throne of grace, that we may obtain mercy, and find grace to help in the time of need." Grace is the enabling power of God to complete your assignment.

110

Many are afraid to shoot their shot because of what they've done. "For all have sinned and fall short of the glory of God" (*NIV*, Romans 3:23). Pick your head up and shoot your shot. God is giving you your confidence back. I command the spirit of condemnation to lose its hold on you. "But because of his great love for us, God, who is rich in mercy, [5] made us alive with Christ even when we were dead in transgressions—it is by grace you have been saved" (Eph. 2:4-5). . Grace saves us, but it does not mean you can continue pursuing wrong.

The Bible asks, "What shall we say then? Shall we go on sinning so that grace may increase? By no means! We are those who have died to sin; how can we live in it any longer?" (Rom. 6:1-2).

"Surely the arm of the Lord is not too short to save, nor his ear too dull to hear" (Isaiah 59:1).

"Come, all you who are thirsty, come to the waters; and you who have no money, come, buy and eat! Come, buy wine and milk without money and without cost" (Isaiah 55:1).

Don't allow your past relationships to rob you of your shot.

You can trust God with your life. The Bible says, "Trust in him at all times, you people; pour out your hearts to him, for God is our refuge" (Psalm 62:8). You can find safety in Him. Many don't feel safe enough to pour their heart out to God. They have become prone to pouring their heart out in the wrong people. David trusted God, so he was willing to allow God to search him. David was willing to lay it all on the table. What are you willing to bring to the table? Not everyone can deal with or handle what you bring to the table, but Jesus can.

SHOOT *your* **SHOT**

About Author

Pastor John Cobb is the Lead Pastor and Founder of The Turning Point Ministries in Birmingham, AL. He is a native of Birmingham, AL. On October 22, 2017, The Turning Point was birth through prayer and fasting. Pastor Cobb is first and foremost a family man. He's a revivalist, intercessor, innovator, entrepreneur, and a strong apostolic prophetic voice in the earth. He is respected and highly sought after for his powerful revelatory teaching and preaching. His ministry is marked by the evident demonstration of the supernatural presence and power of God. He has committed his life to serve and helping people turn their hearts back to God regardless of where they are in life. Pastor Cobb has appeared on The Word Network with the Greg Davis Show, New York WBLS 107.5, Kingdom Choices Broadcasting Network, & V94.9(That's My Pastor). Pastor Cobb is first and foremost a family man. He is a devoted husband to Alexandria Cobb and a proud father of three beautiful children Isaiah, Joel, and Destini.

Made in United States
Orlando, FL
11 December 2021

11517285R00070